Colors

To Flavia

Please visit our web site at: www.garethstevens.com
For a free color catalog describing Gareth Stevens' list of high-quality books and
multimedia programs, call 1-800-542-2595 (USA) or 1-800-461-9120 (Canada).
Gareth Stevens Publishing's Fax: (414) 332-3567.

Library of Congress Cataloging-in-Publication Data available upon request from publisher.
Fax (414) 336-0157 for the attention of the Publishing Records Department.

ISBN 0-8368-2844-5

This edition first published in 2001 by
Gareth Stevens Publishing
A World Almanac Education Group Company
330 West Olive Street, Suite 100
Milwaukee, WI 53212 USA

This edition © 2001 by Gareth Stevens, Inc. Original edition published in French by
Les éditions de la courte échelle inc., Montréal, Canada, under the title *Les couleurs* © 1997
Les éditions de la courte échelle. Additional end matter © 2001 by Gareth Stevens, Inc.

Design concept: Derome Design, Inc.
English translation: Patricia Lantier
English text: Dorothy L. Gibbs and Heidi Sjostrom
Cover design: Scott Krall

Printed in the United States of America

1 2 3 4 5 6 7 8 9 05 04 03 02 01

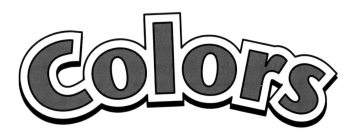

Roger Paré

Gareth Stevens Publishing
A WORLD ALMANAC EDUCATION GROUP COMPANY

The back of a big **blue** whale is the best place to bathe without being bitten by bugs.

This large **yellow** lion
is king of the jungle,
so he eats and he
sleeps as he pleases.

Perched high atop
Bill Bingle's bus full of
pets, a **pink** flamingo
points the way.

Freddie the frog and his best friend, Irene, are out for a stroll, and they're both dressed in **green**.

A big **brown** bear and her cute little cub fiddle the time away, almost each and every day.

An elephant so elegant
in pretty **purple** socks
prances through the
countryside amidst
the hollyhocks.

A clever clown has the skill and the poise to balance on a slippery ball of bluish-green **turquoise**.

An **orange** striped tiger
with its mouth open
wide gobbled all of
our favorite fruit.

Pretty Kitty looks pert
in her **rose**-colored
skirt as she dances
with Max to the music.

Roscoe the rabbit is ready to throw three ripe, **red** apples — one with his toe!

More Books on Colors

Brown Bear, Brown Bear, What Do You See? Bill Martin, Jr. and Eric Carle (Henry Holt)

The Color Kittens. Margaret Wise Brown (Golden Books)

Colors. Little Mouse's Learn-and-Play (series). Anaël Dena (Gareth Stevens)

A First Book about Colors. Look and Learn (series). Nicola Tuxworth (Gareth Stevens)

I Went Walking. Sue Williams and Julie Vivas (Harcourt Brace)

Lunch. Denise Fleming (Henry Holt)

 # Web Sites

Colouring Book.
www.familychannel.ca/f_stuff/games/cbook/frank01.htm

A Rainbow of Frogs.
www.meddybemps.com/9.500.html